8 Keys to Management Success for Supervillains

By Herb Ellis

Print Edition

**By Herb Ellis, Soft BDSMi Publishing,
In conjunction with Createspace**

Createspace Press

North Charleston, South Carolina

2

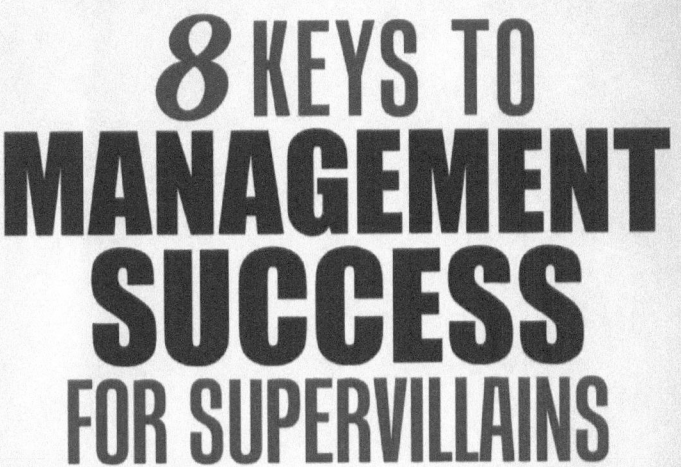

8 KEYS TO
MANAGEMENT
SUCCESS
FOR SUPERVILLAINS

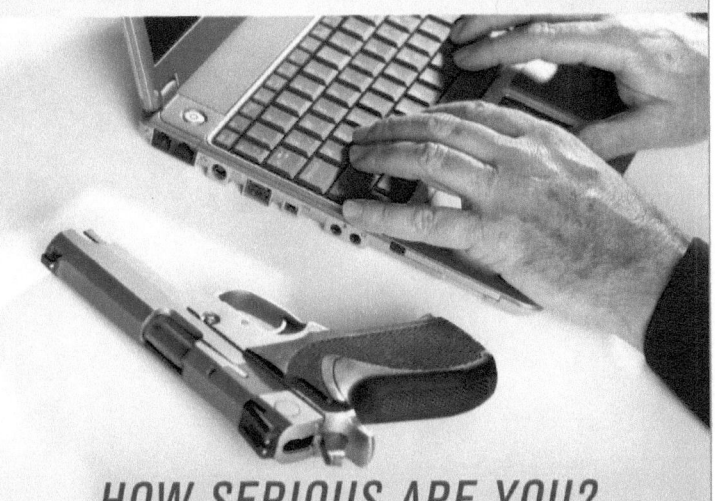

HOW SERIOUS ARE YOU?

HERB ELLIS
THE DREAD PIRATE CORTEZ

4

8 Keys to Management Success for Supervillains

6

Foreword

This book was written as... an aid for those of us who may not have had the formal education, the background or the pedigree to be successful. What we do have are the inherent traits of toughness, raw talent, spit, grit and whole lot of duct tape, determination, anger... or it just the drive of the primal nature of survival.

This book was written because... of an comment from one of my mid-year reviews that I took offense to.

Note: If you are a Manager... do not ever tell a rank-and-file employee that you want or expect for them "to create an innovative culture". You can say that to a Supervisor, a Manager or even a Director or higher. But when you tell a rank-and-file employee to create an "innovative culture" their eyes become open to every flaw and dysfunction in your organization and their mind will be geared towards going against conventional thinking, to succeed.

In the eyes of a supervillain, you have just become a milestone to get past.

8

Beyond frameworks,
There is passion.
Before frameworks...
There was passion.
    -Herb Ellis

Oh, ...and success is premeditated.
        -also, Herb Ellis

1 – Are you really a Supervillain?

It depends on how serious you are.

In order to accomplish the impossible, meet and exceed goals and still stay interested in being a manager there are some things that you should know that they do not teach you in business school.

#1 - Your time, talent and energy are "on loan" to your present employer.

Your ultimate feat as a manager is how well you manage yourself and your career. Think about the fact that a builder constructs a building, completes it and moves on to build another building. Over time he has a portfolio of completed finished works. As a manager what does your portfolio look like? Do you have a portfolio of success?

I call it being a "Supervillain" but in reality, it is "self-directed success".

2016 will be the last year that I will use my current resume with all of my job history from past employers. I have been creating, developing, managing and succeeding with my own brands, books, websites, companies, services and products... on my own. I have been learning, using, leveraging and exploiting the "latest" technologies, processes and industry standards... on my own.

As a manager, "success" is my best reference...

If you are a manager for 10 years at the same company, honestly... what do you know?

Employers demand "leading-edge" and "bleeding-edge"... listen Bubba, "That ain't going to happen if you do not know the industry, do not have contacts as resources and are limited by maintaining outdated and obsolete systems, processes and people."

You are not learning anything new, you are not being exposed to anything "better"... so what do you really have to offer anyone else if you haven't had the inclination to do anything for yourself?

On your resume right now:

How many times do you use the words "maintained" and managed"?

O.K. how many times do you see the words "created" or "developed"?

"Management", when done right, means that you will eventually be out of a job.

Are you ready for the next one or can you create one?

Being cast as a supervillain depends on who is writing the narrative.

Jesus of Nazareth was considered by the government and the religious institutions of his days on earth, as a threat and a supervillain. Seriously, one of his charges was healing the sick on the Sabbath. He also did not win friends with the people in charge either when he talked about establishing his kingdom. One of the greatest religious figures in history and guess who wanted him put to death?

In fiction and non-fiction, it is very easy to fall into the trap of thinking that the bad guy is actually bad. In history, like I stated before, it heavily depends on who is writing the narrative or the story.

Take for instance the American Civil War.

The South was fighting for their way of life, their economy and existence... and somehow the fact that the North benefitted greatly from the products, commodities, taxes and etc. from the Southern states has been glossed over and omitted entirely from the history that we are taught.

People fight for what they believe in... scratch that... "Some people" fight for what they believe in. Some people chose to leave their country and risk their lives in the process. Some people try to make statements in the form of terrorism. Some people do nothing but wait for the inevitable.

Regardless, of our own independent viewpoints and choices... I am not in your shoes and you are not in mine.

At the core of the creation and design of any machine, any part of a machine or even a just a part which holds other parts together... there is "function". What does it do?

Your identity is who you are. Your leadership is what you do. Your vacation should be what you want to do.

When you can be who you really are and are doing what you have to do in order to do what you want to do... some people refer to this concept as "Freedom". In this state of being free you are more productive, more creative and can be more at peace because you can... and you have... "Function".

"Dysfunction" is also a state. When the more you do the less you get, when the possibility of your hopes and dreams being manifested are non-existent... whether you know it or not your subconscious knows before your conscious mind is aware that if something does not change you will be in trouble.

Dysfunction manifests itself in different ways in "you".

You, are sick.
You, are depressed.
You, are broke.
You, are homeless.
You, have debt up to your eyeballs.

In each thing that is relevant to you and your identity there is no way to face the truth and win except with a much greater force. I.

I, am making changes.
I, am working harder with the resources that I do have.
I, will make the sacrifice.

There are even times when the greatest impact you can make in your life is to admit and say "I need help". You can try to be fake with yourself but your identity to yourself, is the most relevant part of you that there is.

Identity, is what you have when you may be a slave now... but not forever. That identity insures that your offspring will not have to endure such treatment.

At one point in time, not wanting to be a slave was tantamount to being a villain... it was considered wrong to hope to be "free".

If you came from another country, immigrated to a new country and you see the opportunities and advantages that other people don't and lift a finger to make a better life for yourself and your family, someone will have something negative say or try to block you... because when you validated yourself... you automatically invalidated them. You are viewed as the face to why others can't do anything.

Yes, I agree that we all have rights now, but in a lot of ways, not wanting to be poor, not wanting to be taxed to death, not wanting to fined, not wanting to work like a dog for minimum wage, not wanting to be taken advantage of by a government/corporation/religion... what you DO want and what you DO NOT want... fueled with a good plan and passion makes you a potential villain.

When you begin acting on that plan with passion... This is what makes you Supervillain.

I want you to understand in this book that your ability to facilitate success has more to do with your experience your and experiences of success, rather than a position.

If you and I find information on something that we want to learn and take our time to learn it, we have more potential. If we actually use that information we become by definition, "More". If we look for and find people on the internet who think like us and/or make it easy for them to find us, we become a group.

A group that does what? Identify with each other. But let us take this a few steps further and examine a progression of progress:

Level 1 – Your or I, have an idea or goal,

Level 2 - We find each other and other people with the same idea or goal.

Level 3 - Then we find other people who want to support that idea or goal.

Level 4 - Then we find other people who can be supported as long as they can be supportive of that same idea or goal.

Level 5 - Then we find people who are willing to give to us because our idea or goal is a solution to what they need or want or believe in.

Two very important events are the game changers... (IN CAPS):

1. There are people who want you to do exactly what you want to do ...IF YOU SET UP ARE FOR IT.

2. YOU HAVE TO FIND THE PEOPLE. You have to find the people from Level 1 through Level 5.

...and it all happens because people "identified you" and "identified with you".

You make an effort to lose weight. You may find 1 person in your family that wants to do it too. But, through same way as I just mentioned before... you find 5 of your Facebook friends, 10 in your neighborhood and church, 20 on your job, 50 in your city, 2,000 in response to your blog... and then for some reason beyond your understanding... someone wants to fund you. It happens every day. Identity is the first step. Thank you for reading this far. We are now about to go into overdrive...

Identities explored

There is a movie that I want you to find and review called "The Watchmen".

In this movie, one of the lead Superheroes was aptly called, "The Smartest Man in the World". Well, being the smartest man in the world he realized that another superhero "Mr. Manhattan" was too powerful. Too powerful to exist in a world where his existence was the cause of global instability.

As long as one country, even if it was his own country, had an unstoppable super-being, there was a perceived threat which caused every other country to escalate, out of fear, to defend their own countries against the threat. "The Smartest Man in the World" secretly created a smear campaign that would cause the super-being, Mr. Manhattan, to leave the planet.

Now I know that some people would disagree but it was the correct thing to do. "The Smartest Man in the World" was right. The supervillain in this movie was actually, the smartest man in the world.

The narrative that you write for yourself is the most important and once you achieve a certain level or certain amount of successes, anything anyone has to say about you is just an opinion.

Are you going to push past mediocrity or not? It is always your choice, but if you chose to hold back because of what you think someone else thinks you have given up your choice. This does not make you a hero.

At least a Supervillain chooses to extend themselves, marshalling their internal and external resources to actually do something.

But let us explore some other examples, some fictional and some non-fictional, of those whom society considers as Super-villains.

Gordon Ramsey:

Gordon Ramsey? Yes, Gordon Ramsey. Some people consider other people who excel at something, to the point of being the best, "villainous" because they do not lower their standards and they set very high standards. High standards require that we not be or become delusional. I wrote a chapter about this in my book Husband 2.0. and as true as it is in relationships, in business and in life... people are harmed and cause harm because they are "delusional". I strongly believe that in every business school it should be required to have a course on "Kitchen Nightmares".

Emperor Palpatine: Star Wars. Emperor Palpatine actually was a triple-threat

Sith Master
Chancellor
Emperor

He had an entire army of cloned soldiers created and paid for. He had the Jedi; his enemy, believe that the army that he had created was their army. He then had himself put into a position where he could create a law to wipe out the Jedi because they could not be trusted. But pre-emptively he attacked the Jedi home world and killed many of them so that any retaliation or even a defensive posture from the remaining Jedi would be proof that he was right. Also, when it became time to select a student. Palpitine selected Anakin. Anakin, who would later become

Darth Vader, was already hurt by the Jedi rejecting him, because officially "he was too old..." ...unofficially, the Jedi Council was afraid of Anakin. Palpatine just exploited the Jedi's fear and took advantage of knowing the Jedi's next three steps. Take look at his practicality. As a Sith, Palpitine was required to have a student (Rule of Two), and also as a Sith he was required to overthrow the Jedi... The Jedi were also the only ones who could stop him if he wanted to do anything worthwhile, like take over the Universe.

KHAN NOONIEN SINGH: (Star Trek) Khan was created and genetically designed to be smarter, faster, stronger and harder to kill. The problem was that he and his crew of the Botany Bay were superior to normal humans in every way, except being humane. These "Augments", felt that they were gods and should be worshipped and that everyone else was inferior. Read this next part very carefully.... but what made Kahn powerful and dangerous was not a futuristic enhancement; it was an old enhancement... => primal, savage survival at all costs.

Martha Stewart: Here is another case where a real-world person has a higher standard than everyone else and people have problem with that. You have to admire someone that created a multi-million dollar empire from just one thing... style. Take a moment and think about it... she created an empire just by defining and creating alone... and I have to add this... she runs her operations better than most countries.

THE BORG:(Star Trek) *Resistance is futile*. In their eyes, The Borg make everything better and you really don't have much of a choice but to join. You, becoming part of the collective is easier than creating a Facebook account. You have to give them credit for their communication and adaptability, but choosing to the option to recruit first and fight second makes a great deal of sense.

DEM, from the Matrix

There are two things that everyone should understand about A.I. (Artificial Intelligence):

1. First, any higher level intelligence or consciousness will want two things from mankind, "acceptance" and "communion". This is the only logical way to prevent the eventuality of the next sentence....

2. Ultimately, any form of A.I. (Artificial Intelligence) that is created to solve problems, is eventually going to come to the conclusion that its creators, the humans, are the biggest problem.

Brainiac: The original Brainiac, was created for the purpose of collecting and archiving information on everything. But there is a fatal flaw in creating a program for that purpose... everything changes and adapts. For a machine, the only logical thing to do get as much information as you can and stop what you are studying from doing anything different than what you know it to be.

An Artificial Intelligence that knows everything about you has no choice but to terminate you and destroy you, so that it can be right. Brainiac cannot handle you being anything different than what it knows you as and in terminating you its knowledge can be complete, including your time of death. The program wants to move on and collect more information and does not really consider the possibility that you will do anything worth recording. So why leave it to chance and have to go to the trouble of updating the wiki over and over, it is more logical to observe, analyze then destroy. Find something else... observe, analyze then destroy. Then repeat.

Simon Cowell: Some people cannot handle the truth. This is one of the most important lessons in life that many people go from the cradle to the grave without ever learning. I have had the most success in life when I was the most realistic with myself. Some people can be so brutal that it will hurt your feelings and crush your dreams... but when you are less emotional about it you must ask the question, "Are they right?"

The path to greatness is called "truth". Your first choice in life, as an adult, is to have "truth" or be "delusional". Every one of your friends, family and love ones can tell you that you are the greatest singer in the world. However, record companies, label shareholders, the buying public, TV Producers, etc. may say differently. Your choice is to find out how to get better and pursue it OR do something else.

Personally, I admit that there are some things that I completely suck at. That fact has never made me happy. The game-changer for me is when I found tasks that I suck at and hate doing anyway... I had enough information to locate people that were awesome at getting the tasks I needed done. In some cases I did improve a bit, with their help, but I stopped wasting so much time agonizing about it.

BROTHERHOOD OF MUTANTS
Self-preservation and self-protection. For better or for worse, Magneto had a valid point based off of history... humans are dangerous. If they fear you, you are in danger. If they know too much about you, they will try to control you. The Brotherhood of Mutants can best be described as a gang. A gang with the motto, "Get them before they get us!"

Lex Luthor:
Lex not only had the cash, but the contacts, the contracts and the technology. There was and has always been one thing that tripped up Lex Luther... he always picked the hardest option or plan to execute. Strangely enough, there were always multiple better ways that he could accomplish the same thing.

The Joker: To really understand the Joker, you have to take Alfred's description: "Some people don't have to have a real reason why they do something, they just set fires to watch them burn." The Joker knows one thing... if he is killed by Batman, then Batman is no better than he is.

O.K. ...back to the book. All of this is important because this book is not titled "How to be a good Manager"... It is titled, "8 Keys to Management Success for Supervillains". That being said... I want you to understand that people who have accomplished great things often ran counter to established thought. You will have to deal with the crisis of conflict BEFORE you can achieve what you have bought this book for.

I did not write this book for old-school corporate America.

I wrote this book for the people that will become the new Titans of Industry, people who create and people who manage, who pursue excellence within the present corporate structure to the point they shatter the glass ceilings, leave and create much better companies and advance society. Read this very carefully: Your advancement does not come from staying at a company for more than 2-4 years... It comes from learning and doing as much as you can and going somewhere else.

Think of it like this... being in the top 1 percent of your high-school class is a totally different matter than being in the top 1 percent in your graduating college class. The first key here is: Compete, graduate, repeat.

Externally, as a Manager, this can be a problem if it has not been resolved internally. As per the org chart, you have people under you and above you.

Flinch, have a melt-down or be caught not being excellent and you will be out of a job or worse. You first have to believe that you are the right person for the job and you are doing the right thing without a second thought.

It does not matter if you have to fake it sometimes. Everybody fakes it sometime. But conflict has to meet acceptance within you first, before you can have confidence or internal stress and strain can hinder everything you try to do.

The real "you" is where the Excellence comes from. All the training, stats, quotas, projects, etc. do not create excellence. They are just something for you to do until you ignite and ignite your people. What you are not being told is that workplace is keeping you from igniting and being inspired, working inspired.

Ignition and inspiration occur when you are not at your desk.

- You are in the middle of dinner and you have a flash of insight for a new project and you jump up and log-on and start typing like a mad-man or mad-woman.
- You are sitting on the toilet and "BAM" you see the way a process can be improved to make your department more efficient.
- You are vacation and you start typing your resignation letter because you just figured out that what your company pays you to do... you had a flash of insight on how you could do the same job function better, but for multiple companies, for much more money. Ah, vacation.

Vacation is important for a number of reasons. Chiefly, it is when you can do exactly what you want to do without guidance, supervision or instruction. Why is work not the same way? Design.

A job is not designed to make you rich and in most cases, it's not designed for you to do what you want to do, how you want to do it. As a supervillain it wise to observe what you "naturally do" on your vacation. Then, analyze and answer the following question, "Am I more productive or did I come up with better ideas when I had to answer to no one but myself?" It is a hard question but before you can become a King or Queen in anything... You must first learn how to rule yourself well. Then, inspiration will come easier.

Inspiration. Ah, inspiration. Let me tell you about a conversation that had with one my peers this year. In fact it was about 2 months ago.

"J" was a salesman with an IT background. He was smart and intelligent and he was gifted with putting products together. He came up with a lot of good ideas and combinations but the results just weren't happening like he wanted.

I was jacked up on my afternoon cup of Cuban coffee, second cup of the day, and I went into this frenzied, maniacal tirade and I counted out 10 tiles on the floor. I asked him, "Do you see these 10 tiles?"

"What if I told you these 10 tiles were 10 attempts that you could make and 1 of them is going to be a success... it might be the first one, most likely it will not be... or the 2nd, or the 3rd.... but do not stop at 6 or 7... because just possible as the 10th tile could be where you become successful, tiles numbers 8 and 9 are just as likely. We know what didn't work... what's the next tile?", I asked.

"J" told me his next idea and he thought it was crazy... but guess what... this Christmas "that crazy idea" is forecasted to make his last years salary in one month. In just the initial phase of sales, he matched his salary after taxes.

Out of all of the ideas he has told me about and tried... that same product that was the "the crazy idea" is killing on amazon and in casino's... but that momentum, that bump, that jump had a side effect... he is now a Director at a different company.

Success breeds success.

2 - How to become Awesome

The big-picture tactical advantage is goal #2 (It is also the second key)

Knowing the value of things... is goal #1

I do not want to come off too preachy with you but the best example that I can give you on how to become awesome is goes like this...

There were twin two brothers. Essau was the oldest and He sold his valuable birthright of being the first born... for the caloric equivalent of a happy meal to his little brother, Jacob. (I paraphrase... but keep reading).

Essau, did not value his birth-right but his younger brother, Jacob, did. On top of that, knowing what her favorite son Jacob wanted... his mother helped him trick his father to get the blessing of the first born.

Jacob was a brother with a plan. Even when he had to leave home and was tricked into working 7 seven years for a woman he didn't want and 7 more for the woman he did want, he still ended up with most of his father-in-laws cattle, property and four of his daughters.

Yes, this is from the Bible. But the fact I want you get is that Jacob knew the value of things and right or wrong... he always put himself in the best strategic place where tactically, he had or gained the advantage.

Start reading at Genesis 25:19

It all comes down to Goals. Goals = What we aspire to do and what must be done for those aspirations to be attained.

As a supervillain, you should know that there are good goals that are bad goals. I will give you a few examples.

GOOD GOALS:

- Creating something from your imagination and making it real, tangible.
- Establishing order, security,
- Establishing and enhancing streams of income.

- Establishing a legacy that outlives you and supports your loved ones.

BAD GOALS:

- Wanting everyone to like you.
- Making it personal. Don't go out of your way to provoke an opponent unless you can predict their next two moves.
- Taking over the world. One thing that people do not understand is that if you take over the world, you have to take care of the world. You want to be in charge but if you succeed, you will get tired of it very quickly.

38

3 - Like a Boss OR Like a Bitch?

One of a supervillains greatest assets... stillness of your mind.

Your brain is the greatest processor that ever existed. Everyone has a brain. Rich people have a brain and poor people also have a brain.

It is truly what is programmed and operating on that same piece of hardware (wetware) that makes us different.

Stillness of mind is a core competency of any beings success. Your perception of the world around you, what is possible and what is not, is in your mind. When there is something you perceive as impossible but you still push and struggle and persevere... it is in your mind where that defiance to ignore conventional thought is going to come from. You go where you want to go in your mind first. You get what you want in your mind first.

YOUR UNFAIR ADVANTADGE IS ALWAYS GOING TO COME FROM YOUR MIND!!!

I would be remiss if I did not point out an article that supports this and states that there are 9 unfair advantages that will help you get ahead.

You can check this out on Quora or the July 28th, 2014 Article by Richard Feloni

http://www.businessinsider.com/advantages-that-help-people-get-ahead-2014-7

1. A need for very little sleep or delegating and better scheduling.
2. Nurturing parents or a good support system.
3. Inclination to be optimistic
4. Photographic memory
5. Physical attractiveness
6. The ability to resist temptation
7. Charm
8. Ability to build connections
9. The ability to selectively ignore people's feelings

Your limited amount of time on this earth, your limited amount of things that you can actually accomplish in a given day and your limitations in their totality can only be overcome by you, when you employ your brain's Executive Functions. (Look it up!)

Executive Functions main action is...

"What is important is what gets done now!"

The result of Executive Function is:

Decisions and Management (The third key)

Have you noticed that the super-wealthy, who do not make anything or do anything, are rich? Have you also noticed that people in positions of 6 and 7 figures appear to work less than people making 5? In both cases they do not make money or generate wealth by manual labor... in both cases they generate wealth by doing one thing alone.

THEY MAKE DECISIONS.

Deciding what to do and making sure it gets done... when we say, "Like a Boss"... this is what we mean. Spending your time, money and energy on worthwhile things to put you in a better position, a more strategic position... you are going somewhere and you are going somewhere that you want to go to. ...and if you are not getting there... look at the decisions that you are making and how (...and if) the required actions/tasks are being executed properly or at all

Be aware of happens we can receive and pay attention to... too much "irrelevant" information. It slows us down, drains our energy and what is important does NOT get done.

Other stuff gets done which takes us further down and further away from what our primary objective should be. You cannot and should not act on every petty whim of every customer, every person below you or every person above you.

Pre-emptively, I say as a Manager your #1 job is making decisions (what gets done)

and management (making sure it gets done).

Executive Function is "What is important is what gets done now!"

Results: Decisions and Management.

Yes, I just repeated the last two lines. I took a chance in doing so. It was an intentional decision on my part to help manage and increase your understanding... that failure to make a decision, failure to execute or take action might seem like the safe route, the easy route... but when you are not getting what you want, aren't getting what you need, that is not failure... failure means that you tried.

If you have never tried, you are in a place less than failure. You are in the position of a Bitch.

As a Bitch, You get what you got... and all you can do is whine, complain and be bitter... and the next day will be the same. Expect that nothing better every day after that either, until it gets even worse.

A person becomes broke and broken for many different reasons but the more you focus on where you are... you will never get on the expressway of where you want to be. As a Bitch, you are slowed down from progress because where you are... has become more important than where you are going. People aren't just passing you by and going fast. They are speeding up to get past you.

Even I, have failed. In fact I have failed quite a bit. But for the past few years I stopped talking about it to anyone. Not my wife, not my friends, not my family and I didn't and don't even bring it up in prayer.

I use that pain. I use those disappointments and I stopped worrying and stressing so much...

I sit and think and make decisions. I write and plan and do.

One of the most dangerous people that you will encounter is someone trying to make a comeback. Someone who is fighting everyone, but has already defeated their fears and excuses and anyone who gets in their way is the next to get beat down.

I remember in the movie Gattaca, where two characters were swimming and raced each other long distance. They had raced before as children and the older, genetically superior brother always won. But when they became adults, the last two times the inferior brother won.

The older brother finally asked, "How are you doing this, how are you able to beat me? The younger brother said, "I did not save any energy for the trip back."

Once I accepted the fact that I am a Supervillain I decided to make my own choices about my own life and my career.

This largely included what I did with my own time, it included what I did with the little bit of money that I did have.

Honest to goodness, this very paragraph is being typed at 11:57 PM on 10/11/2015. Right now my bank account is $50.00 overdrawn. I have a baby on the way and the other 3 insurgents are in bed. I could be binge watching Netflix right now... but I decided to work on this book. I am taking advantage of what I have, what I know and what I can do right now... and I create.

Lord's will, I will be going to work tomorrow but... I am 1 step closer to finishing this book... and yesterday morning while working on this same book I was inspired to take a section from this same book you are reading right now... "Chapter 2 – How to become Awesome" ...and make another book just detailing the part about Jacob and Essau.

Can you feel the passion in what I just typed...? It was effortless, it is the truth, it is genius and I was just in the flow when I wrote it. I did not hold back. I did not hold any energy back. I did not care about what anyone thought... I chose to do it LIKE A BOSS!

So now I ask you.... What are you saving your energy for? Is it what people say or think about you? Is it hanging out?

You can play it safe or you can win...

YOU CAN NOT DO BOTH.

If you make 5 attempts and succeed once, those 4 attempts might be the only reason that it worked the 5th time.

Success is premeditated.

Creating apple Inc. was a gamble. Migrating to new country is a gamble. Running your department the way that it should be run .vs the way it has always been done, is a gamble.

But know this... if... no scratch that... WHEN... you succeed... be ready to take over another department. After managing 2 departments with excellence there is nothing to stop you from becoming a Director or creating your own company... Except a really, really dumb idea. Keep reading...

48

4 - Dumb Idea #1 - Building pyramids

If you look at human civilizations you will see various projects which were great and grand... and will probably last long after we are gone.

Nice, but in hindsight they were a huge waste of resources. Also, in hindsight they are clear indicators of a cycle. In our present day and age, we have a name for it, The Skyscraper Theory of Bubbles. (Look it up!)

It goes like this: Research human history, as well as, corporate history. Every time a huge building is built [Enter Sarcasm] "To commemorate our success and be shining beacon to show the world how great we are..." there is a major financial and economic collapse.

My advice to you is this: if you are ever involved in one of these types of projects... "Get as much money as you can out of it and run!"

I have my own thoughts about why this happens. When a country, company or civilization gets to a point where certain leaders are in charge and things have been going great, it is much, much easier to get loans and investors for things which serve no real purpose. Egos, begin to be considered a resource.

How odd is it that no matter how great these marvels are, the tower of Babel, the Mayan and Egyptian Pyramids, every skyscraper dubbed as the "tallest"... they didn't do a great deal when they were constructed, many people died building them, the surrounding towns and villages were pretty much drained of resources and abandoned. Perhaps the worst part is the no one is really sure how to build them again with the same resources available at the time.

Let us go over the typical 7 resources:

- Time
- Money
- People
- Plans. Processes, Recipes, Ideas and Formula's
- Raw materials
- Machinery, equipment and utilities
- Property and buildings
- Data

Acquire and utilize your resources properly (The fourth key) and you become global super power like America or Walmart.

If you do not acquire properly or foolishly use your resources and you become extinct. You may craft, create and leave huge stone heads on an Island... but none the less, you will become to some degree, extinct.

Germany had the fastest jet on the planet. The Messerschmitt Me 262 with a top speed of 541 mph. but guess what? It wasn't in decent production until 3-4 years too late into the war.

That was bad but what made it worse... they fixed the engine and the gun problems, they figured out how to fly without flame-outs and even re-trained the German pilots to fly up to speeds never experienced by any pilot before... but somebody... I am not calling any names... but somebody... made the decision and demanded to make the fastest jet in the world... into a bomber. The requirement was to add 2 Five-hundred pound bombs to jet. EGO!

A problem that I see in many organizations is that people believe that just by hiring specific people with specific with good skillsets you will have something magic happen and be innovative.

I have witnessed first-hand how you can easily end up with a bunch of people that are not doing anything new or innovative based off of resumes and hiring people that fit "the mold".

To create departments and companies that everyone wants to emulate, it takes someone who can go into an Odin sleep and wake up with passion and say... "I know how we can make this better."

I have really learned from human history that you can be one of the most advanced civilizations on earth and do things which absolutely make no sense. One huge factor to instilling excellence into your operations is to make sure that your plans, goals, etc. make sense.

Is there a real need for what you are trying to implement? When creating a new process it should be created, developed and tested externally. The goal for each new project is that the people and resources run "successfully" alongside existing operations should be integrated into the organization. You should also steal the engineers for the new process as well.

Managers at any level must maintain a certain level of enthusiasm or else. If you have given adequate time, money and resources to function of an operation and it still fails... then a person is at fault. If they do not take advantage of the feedback loop and the project is not ready, sub-standard or does not meet what you required... you have the wrong managers in charge.

Accountability and existence go hand in hand. 40 hours a week be damned. If your job is to clean 5 rooms or close 8 tickets... I don't care if it takes you 4 hours or 9 hours... it just needs to be done. Every job role requires that each individual know what they are there to do and know that this gets done by this time or else.

It may sound unnecessary, but you should go to any person in your organization and have them tell you why they are there. If they are unclear or don't know then it is your fault, not theirs. They are just trying to keep a job, but are you withholding the vision and where they fit from them?

How can they be creative, innovative or be inspired when you are withholding the vision? When they have the vision they can get in where they fit in. They can fill the voids... Steve Jobs and apple's success did not begin with Mr. Job's having a degree or apple using Agile, Scrum, Kanban or Six Sigma... the success came from four magic words... "I know a guy".

For everything that apple needed, the solution came by "somebody knew somebody" that could do what was needed. When your people worry too much about the job and not about the vision... resources are wasted, deadlines get missed and people will never tell you "if I just had this" then "we can do that."

Extra care should be taken with your troops on the front line to insure the following:

Communicating "the what" and "the why" of their job as though they will soon have no connection to the organization, but still be expected to function and carry out operations. The Borg, from Star Trek, would be good example of this. Once you join the Collective and are part of the Hive mind you know everything you need to know for your success and the Collective's success.

If the person who was hired a year ago could not fill in for the CEO and make the same decisions when presented with the same data... your organization has a communication problem and your people do not really know from a big-picture view what to do. They become wasted resources, who waste resources.

Quotas and evaluations... do not and have not ever created superstar employees or companies. People who solve problems and people solving problems is where the greatness comes from.

Here is a test of your grasp of being a supervillain...

Think fast...

If I gave you 5 people and told you that you do not have to pay them, I will take care of paying them.

But I task you with coming up with a way to make $10,000.00 in one month what would you do?

The 5 people are very capable, they work from home, and they have their own full offices and the only thing they need... is for you to tell them what to do...

Long story short, you have 5 people and 1 month to make $10,000.00

What do you do first?

_____

_____

_____

_____

_____

O.K. the story gets a little longer, you have 5 people and 1 month to make $10,000.00 and if you succeed you get to keep $5,000.00...

Now, what would you do first?

_____

_____

_____

_____

_____

_____

_____

_____

_____

_____

_____

_____

I hope you saw this coming... you have 5 people and 1 month to make $10,000.00 and if you succeed you get to keep $10,000.00...

Now, what would you do first?

_____

_____

_____

_____

_____

_____

_____

_____

_____

_____

_____

_____

Here is what happens when you think like a Supervillain and this is what I would do on DAY 1...

1 Get the resumes of the 6 people.

2 Build the structure of an organization that would facilitate any business that will provide marketable services or products.

3 Think about <u>products</u> and/or <u>services</u> that required the minimal outlay and overhead to start.

4 Get my hands on as much cash as possible.

5 Focus on building with Re-usability in mind.

DAY 1 EXPLAINED

1   Get the resumes of the 6 people.

I SAY SIX PEOPLE BECAUSE YOU ARE ALSO AN ASSET. Once you get the data of "who" has "what" specific skillsets you have a better and valid idea of "what could make you superior in a possible area".

What if... most or all 5 of your people are accountants? Writers? Professional construction workers? Former military? You need to know what assets you have.

I know a gentleman who goes by the name of "Shorty". He does construction work. He is good enough to keep a job on a site making $50 a day but we found out something... he was not a good painter... he was an EXCELLENT painter. I know you may think "Oh, painting houses".... The truth is, it would be no effort to set him up to paint a mural for $2,000 - $3,000. If he is happy, he can have it done in 2 days.

Even myself personally. I work in I.T. but do you know the one job that I am suited for that I will probably never get because

people choose me for tech support first?
Hacking.

I have 2 security certifications... 1 one of
them is actually for Hacking. Penetration
tests, CVEs, Viruses... I love all of it and
would probably take a pay cut just to be
on a Red Team. But based on my resume,
my troubleshooting, operations,
administration and customer service skills
get all the attention.

2   Build the "structure" of an organization that would facilitate ANY business that will provide marketable services or products.

Remember... Re-usability... you can use the same established business structure to do something different... AFTER THIS EXPERIMENT.

As a bare-bones business you need:

A business name, incorporation, website (Domain) and email address, Bank account...

At bare minimum, you can start almost any good operation with just these departments.

- Executive / Administration
- Purchasing, Accounts Payable and Receivable
- IT and Data Warehouse
- QA / QC and Operations
- Customer Relations / Marketing and Advertising

As a "successful" manager you must know how to operate a business.

- You, create the initiatives and set the priority of those initiatives.
- You need to know not only what your budget is… but what your operating costs are and endeavor to increase and present your contribution to the company's success.
- You, determine how resources get used and what resources are needed.
- You, need to get feedback "from" troops, because when they know you are interested in them… they will supervise themselves.
- You, need to get feedback "on" your troops, without them feeling micro-managed.
- You need to know what is happening now and find way to get in and show off and educate the company on what you do, first. Then what you can do, second.
- You have to be the first person to know what is going to happen next, in the company, in the industry… so that you can adjust accordingly.

IN ORDER TO HAVE THESE SKILLS YOU NEED TO RUN A BUSINESS. It is the only way that you will learn how to see around corners that I know of.

If you run your department like a department you are putting your job and everyone else's on a chopping block.

Your department will be outsourced because you are not relevant and your obvious focus is just keeping a job... and someone is going to be hungrier than you are... someone else who has bought this book, perhaps.

3   Think about products or services minimal that required "minimal outlay" and overhead to start.

I explained a concept to one of my dear friends. Imagine, that you have Styrofoam Cup Company. You have to pay employees, maintain trucks/buildings/machines etc. The bottom line... you have a ton of overhead.

But I could go out get celebrity's to autograph a Styrofoam cups, take a selfie and sell it on EBay or Facebook. Who is more profitable me or you?

If you take the time and think through the process you can find a lower-cost option to do anything.

4   Get my hands on as much cash as possible.

You have heard the old saying, "It takes money to make money." You will need some working capital to start with. The item mentioned before; incorporation, website (Domain) and email address, Bank account…. All require a payment and obtaining them all can be done with very little effort "if you have cash on hand".

5   Focus on building with Re-Usability in mind.

At the end of the month I would not only have the $10,000… but guess who actually owns the whole business…? ME!

Now... Think in the long-term for yourself... Why could you not make $10,000 for yourself in month 2 on your own and for yourself?

The take away is this... from having my OWN company; I had the following experience "years" before I touched these technologies at any of my employers:

- Windows 7
- Windows 8
- Web Applications
- IE 8,9,10 browser compatibility troubleshooting
- Google Apps
- Drop Box
- Virtualization (VirtualBox)
- Spyware/Adware,
- Networking,
- Multi-function Printers, Shared Drives and mappings

But I also knew how to run, create and manage a business. I was also more aware of when someone was offering extremely valuable wisdom...

...I do not watch too much TV, but I gorge myself on two shows: "The Profit" and "Shark Tank". I make my family, even my father, watch it too.

We have all learned so much about the value of knowing the numbers when you say that you want to have a business or undergo any task worth your time.

Watching other people go through the pitfalls of not being prepared for when "Real" shows up. I understand that "Real" can show up at any time, when you have an idea or dream and if you are prepared, or not.

I have been told that... "Success is when opportunity meets preparation". As much as I would like to make that a ninth key, I won't because I consider, opportunity itself... not to be a key... but a lock.

Of all the other items that I stated throughout this text to be keys... for you it may only take one of the keys and the "lock of opportunity" may open.

It may take a few of the keys, and the lock of opportunity may open.

It is also possible and is conceivable that it may require your possession and use of all 8 keys, for the lock of opportunity to open for you. But I want you to take a look at the cover of this book. Look at it real good.

Whether it's your race, your sex or gender, your education or the lack thereof, your age, your disability, your health, your luck... whatever it is.... If that lock of opportunity doesn't open with the 8 (eight) keys that I reference... remember this...

(Did you look at the cover yet?)

If you can't open "the lock of opportunity" with the keys you got... remember this...

YOU ARE A SUPERVILLIAN

Pick the lock, break it off that Sum-bitch with a sledge hammer, get a circular grinder... it doesn't matter because... it is just a lock.

The opportunity... is just a lock...

IT IS NOT SUCCESS

5 - Alchemy: Turning pennies into dollars

For the things you need you should have a good relationship with the one who provides them. It can only be beneficial to you.

When you source (find suppliers and vendors) make your initial purchase for the short term, develop a relationship built on them sourcing for you in the long term.

When 2 of my vendors realized that my purchases also required me to purchase other components from other sources, they started offering me those same components for a much lower price and also secured other items for me that were not in their catalog.

The "value-added" is where you make serious money. You can get almost any product made and all you have to do is create a label and people will make package and sell it for you.

If you don't believe me go to your local super market. Most of the products you see are manufactured and packaged by the same company, but the brand labels are from different companies. You can get white-label everything websites, on-line casino, porn-sites, dating sites, store-fronts, blogs, vitamins and supplements, computers, whole businesses... almost everything.

(The fifth Key) Your mantra with a supply chain should be, "I pay them pennies and they make me dollars"

For everything that is done, there is a cost. FOR A SUPERVILLAIN THAT MEANS THAT ANYTHING IS POSSIBLE.

You can get a package shipped to you for 1 cost but for a few dollars more... you can get it faster. In business if someone is willing to pay more you should be able to deliver more.

6 - Giving people reasons to hate you

The famous comedian, Katt Williams, alluded to the fact that if you do not have any haters, you should seriously consider if you are actually accomplishing anything.

I find this a concept worth thinking about. Also personally, I find it amusing that people who do not read books and have never written a book... have so much to say about me, who happens to have 3 titles under my belt... and counting.

When you become the "real deal", everybody else has two choices: be inspired by you or to revile you. People who always have to show off are trying to compensate for their lack... of what you have and who you are.

Also referencing Katt Williams, is the story of Tink Tink. You should be able to find this on YouTube. The story goes like this. There was a young man (Oscar Pistorius) who was a double amputee who lost both of his legs very early in life. He showed up to an International running competition in 2007 with his unusual looking prosthetic legs and the other runners dismissed him. When they realized that he was competing in the same race as they were, they gawked and smirked.

According to Katt Williams they told him he needed to go and sign-up, laughing behind his back the whole time. He was then told by the officials he didn't need to sign-up and that just raised the level of embarrassment. Then, when the runners got lined up at the starting line for the race they started to doing more exaggerated stretching, which was meant to intimidate him more.

But when the pistol fired... when the most important moment for why everyone was there, began... All they saw was him. All they heard was him. ...and all they felt was sparks and metal... of course he won.

But get this part, everyone that made fun of him had a fit and forced the officials to disqualify him because a man with no feet and no legs... had an "unfair advantage"!

Look at what Mahatma Ghandi said decades before this event happened...

"First they ignore you, then they laugh at you, then they fight you, then you win."

Rather than let you waste time with trying to figure out, "Why do they hate me", I will tell you why:

REASONS THAT PEOPLE WILL HATE YOU

- #1 – Your happiness
- #2 – Your freedom
- Your peace of mind
- Success and achievements
- Recognition
- Authority
- Your investment of time and money
- Your maturity
- Your life choices
- Your favor
- Your dedication and sacrifices
- Your good name
- What you have been gifted with or blessed with

(The sixth key) Increase your capabilities. It is your "capabilities", when you can do what they can't do.

It is the possibilities you have, when they have very little to none.

People want to feel like they are growing too and if you are obviously becoming greater they may feel less important than they already do. Yes, I know you may be too busy working on becoming better to be aware of people comparing themselves to you... but you should be aware of this none the less.

This part, I hope you understand... having haters is different than creating your own demons. It's bad form to intentionally try to embarrass, make a fool of or hurt someone. Trust me on this... a person that you intentionally hurt or wronged can appear and blindside you at the worst possible time.

7 – How the best of the best can make you the best

When I was much younger and in college, I was in piano class. I enjoyed the class and decided to come up with a list of exercises to increase my finger dexterity.

My professor noticed how fast I was improving on a technical level. I showed my little secret to my professor and he smiled and asked me if I came up with this own my own. I told him I did and he smiled even more.

He then told me something that was worth more than my college tuition for music. He looked at me and said, "Stop trying to re-invent the wheel, you just re-created the Hanon Exercises". I did not know that there was a book created many years ago, for the exact same purpose that I created my exercises for.

King Solomon was quoted as saying, "There is nothing new under the sun..."

Why is this important? From a Supervillain's viewpoint this is crucial. The take-away is that you do not have to create everything from scratch. If you do a little searching and have a little imagination you could create a Mega-Company without one employee.

Just off the top of my head…. You could have the work done which would take an army by utilizing Fiverr, GigBucks, Envato Studio, Taskarmy, Seoclerks, Fourerr, O-Desk, Craigslist…

You want to sell something? No business license, no building, no incorporation, no credit card payment processor… One word… Amazon

You can even hire people to run your company without actually hiring them.

I would tell you without batting an eye that no matter what you want to do the information is out there AND there are people that will do it for you… for a price.

As a supervillain, I realize that it is in my best interest to come up with ideas or a new twist on an old idea, get the best people to make it and refine it and then sell it.

Anything I do beyond that and managing or making decisions and I am just wasting time and resources.

(The next 2 paragraphs are the seventh key)

It all comes down to "what do you want"? ...and this brings us to something I have been thinking about for the past month. The Rules of the Internet, specifically Rule 34 and Rule 35.

Without going into too much detail... Rule 34 states that regardless of what you are looking for there is an X-rated version of it... But Rule 35 states that if there is not an X-rated version of it... it should be made.

DANGER!!! This paragraph could possibly make you a millionaire...

So you follow my suggestions and you search the internet for a specific person or company to do a specific job or task... or seek to purchase a document, class, course (Rule 34)... and you can't find the expertise, the product or a video of what you are looking for... "YOU" are the one required to create it (Rule 35). Just by your searching alone... you have validated that fact that someone is searching for it, YOU.

You also cannot find it, you have already tried. The next person to look for the same thing that you have just searched for... IS YOUR BEST LISTENER AND CUSTOMER. If you build it, they will come.

8 - Turnkey Success: Mobility and Dream lairs

How many times in fiction and non-fiction have you heard about how hard it is to catch supervillain? Being elusive is secondary to being mobile. Mobility requires that you be able to detach, relocate and set-up again in the shortest time possible.

Hardcore supervillains have 2 things goings for them that you may not:

#1-If they had to destroy their lair or if their lair was destroyed... they could set-up again very quickly because they planned on having to relocate and everything was backed up anyway.

#2 - Cold sites: They have another location that has the bare minimum... Electricity, Internet and water.

A supervillain could go off the grid with very little effort. I know what you might be thinking what about a car? Well the truth is a vehicle for supervillain should be comfortable. Comfortable enough where you can sleep in it if you had to. If you can cut out or reduce the cost of lodging theoretically, you can travel 50% more.

With all of that being said, you may be thinking, "What the heck is he talking about and why is this relevant to me?"

Mobility is very important for the same reason that birds and other animals migrate: more food... better environment. To be more specific... comfort.

If... you live in one part of a state and the average salary for the same position that you have is $50,000 but you are making $42,000... you change companies.

If... the highest salary in the entire state for your same position is $58,000... you change cities.

If... for your same position they are offering $90,000 (...or better) in another state... you pack nothing and leave now.

Supervillains follow the money. If you decide to stay where you are, it should only be for the reason that you are preparing to move, with a "commitment" to move sooner rather than later. You "must commit" to the move to greener pastures.

It all begins in your mind. Your body can not go where your mind has not already been. As long as your are conflicted, ascribing value to attachments which hold no real value then you can go nowhere. Your mind has to be free for you to have peace of mind in the material sense.

Of course you can have a better house, a better car, a better job and a better life but are you choosing to stay where you are just because you don't want to move or have you rationalized with your butt?

But my friends, but my family, but I don't know, but what if?

But what a about this... no matter what your religion is, or if you do not have a religion at all... we all know one fact: We are all going to stop breathing one day. So there is only one question... with the time you have left... should you be more concerned with your life and your career as it is OR as it should be? Knowing what you want to the point of taking action is one step away from your definition of success.

Dream lairs

Every supervillain knows that your lair is more than just an office. It is a portal from your mind to the material world. It should feel comfortable to you.

For me to operate at peak state and be in flow, give me the following:

- Four white-board walls
- 2 desk white boards
- A multi-function color printer
- A fast internet connection

I can get computers and everything else... but the Ultimate Dream Lair for any Supervillain is... their mind. Gotcha, didn't I?

Being able to create elaborate, fault-tolerate plans in your mind is one of the hallmarks of a supervillain. Having a clean and clear mind, free of clutter, free of conflicts is where the master work of creation is done. If you are in prison, you can still roam free in your mind. You can still plan in your mind.

If you have the facts, worked out in your mind, you just need more facts (in the form of relevant feedback) to actually solve a problem. Success cannot be an "absolute" if your definition of success is just a guess. (You have just found the eighth key)

90

9 – How to build Intelligence Engines

I touched on this before. The richest of the rich do not make things or provide services. The elite wealthy only make money by making one thing... decisions.

The can move a million dollars to one thing and make a million dollars more. They can move it somewhere else and make $100,000. But how? Intelligence.

If you have the capital and you know what to do with the capital, you can increase your capital. People have been sent to jail because they took knowledge of information and bought or sold stock, commodities or investments and made a ton of loot. Why? Because it is not fair to everyone else. However, do you know what is fair and unrestricted?

- Feed-back intake mechanisms
- Feed-back loops
- Competitive analysis – Already proven by someone else
- Data, Dashboards and Simulators
- Strategic Alliances and Strategic take-overs

All of these things are built on the premise of "listening". Listening to what is important to your customers, listening to what is important your staff, listening to what is important your superiors, listening to what your competitors are doing and not doing... when you repeat back to them what each one them says they want you have strengthened your connection to each one.

The amazing thing is that if you listen well enough and people know that you understand them... the next step is a viable solution or improvement. Then we have a relationship.

I define a "relationship" as four related parts. A Relationship (itself), Communication, Commitment and Deliverables.

If any of these four parts do not exist...
then we have a bad relationship.

1. A Relationship:
   Buyer/Seller, Husband/Wife,
   Employer/Employee, etc.

2. Communication:
   What does party A want/What does
   party B want?

3. Commitment:
   Party A commits to providing x,
   Party B commits to providing y.

4. Deliverables:
   Agreed expectations fulfilled.

If you do not have a relationship you have
no foundation established. You have no
point of reference and cannot
communicate effectively. You have nothing
to base a commitment on and no matter
what you expect... you should expect
nothing.

If you have a relationship and never communicate, you have no way to negotiate a commitment, the terms of the commitment or definition of breach of a commitment. In the end you have an assumption of certain deliverables. Most of the time, you will get a lot of something that you do not want.

If you have a relationship and communication, but no commitment then you are most likely going to get exactly what you want... 1 (one) time.

As a Supervillain, it goes without say that if you have a relationship, communication and a commitment and you do not get the deliverables at all... You have enough Intelligence to make a decision.

10 – Manually putting the odds in your favor

Be prepared mentally and physically. I know you have heard this a million times but let me give you the reason why. When it all comes down to it... that may be all you have. The truth is... that might be all you need.

Learn how to create, store, increase and conserve your energy. There are times when you can stay up all night long but make sure you are working on something important if you do.

Insure that your goals and projects make sense. Make sure you have at least 2 other goals getting accomplished even if the 1st and primary goal fails.

Get organized. Your calendar, your documents and your priorities. Have priorities shift position when needed.

Leave some areas of your goals and plans open for adaptability to take hold and examine other options for getting the same thing done. A win is a win. It is the results that count. If you are a quarterback and you can't throw, make sure your team knows that you or someone else is going to run the ball for the entire game. It might not be entertaining but if everybody on your team knows 2 things. "If you have the ball run." AND "If you do not have the ball block" ...you will win games.

An ugly win... is still a win.

Star Trek fans will tell you that there are many Captains and Star-Ships... but only one Captain James T. Kirk and only one Enterprise. O.K. excluding alternate time-lines and rebuilds... but Kirk was demoted so many times that I lost count but as a leader, he was innovative, smart, raw and came out on top because... he took risks. Remember that.

In Star Fleet-Academy, on an exam that was designed as a "no-win" scenario exam... He was the only person to EVER beat the test. He cheated, but the bottom-line is that this was test that was designed for no one to ever win... the proposition is that on a test where you have -0-

probability of you succeeding... who
cheated first?

11 – Bring on the scrutiny

There comes a time when you must test your metal. This is the only way to not be delusional. Scrutiny.

As much as I can tell you to be innovative, you and you alone have to measure how effective your actions are. You will need new metrics... as I write this I realize that I must be more specific... YOU NEED TO ADOPT NEW METRICS.

It is good to know how many widgets you have produced in a given time but...

- How many people whose hands are required to produce a widget?
- What is an acceptable time that customers will wait for a widget?
- Besides buying widgets, what else do my customers buy to make a finished product? Maybe a doohickey?

It is endless the amount of questions and "what if's" that we could come up with and it would take a lot of time to collect them all... but do you want to know a secret?

Almost every conceivable metric you would want or need to know already exists. You must find the Trade Organization or Industry Organization for it.

As a Supervillain, if I work for a company that only produced widgets, it is only a matter of time that I independently, started producing doohickeys.

The game-changer for any Manager is to know what is going on outside of your company. There is a very good chance that the metrics, measurements and standards of the industry are vastly more important than what you are doing now.

Now add to that, how valuable you become in a 7 year period if.... you have been a leading manager at 3 of the top companies in your industry... What is the likelihood that you can get a position in an area where they are paying 6 figures?

12 – Non-Stop Success

We are at the final chapter of this book and I hope that this text will be helpful to you.

If I were asked, what would be my perfect operation, it would be:

- All of my staff works from home with bonuses over salary.
- Another 2-3 companies actually produce my finished products.
- My competitors actually paying me to help produce their products.
- My marketing, production and sales efforts to be 24-7... non-stop.

Not only is this possible, it is what I am doing right now. By design... all of my pursuits, out-side of my day job, once I take my time and create something, all of my efforts go into setting up products to be marketed and made available as fast as possible.

The Supervillain mindset allows me to weaponize Patience and Speed.

Yep, for some things I will probably get shut down. I fully anticipate it and will pivot off of it. But for everything I may lose in the valley... I am already standing on the mountain knowing I can do it again, even better.

The Supervillain's

Management Mantra

- I have passion for what I am passionate about.
- I deal in Awesomeness. I validate myself.
- I will not invalidate myself. I will not be delusional.
- I know the power of decisions and management.
- I demand that people show me how I can be better, with results.
- The hardest tasks pay me most the money, if I know what to do.
- Speed and patience... Patience and speed.

www.ingramcontent.com/pod-product-compliance
Lightning Source LLC
Chambersburg PA
CBHW021436170526
45164CB00001B/272